THE WICKED BOOK OF

txtj0x

With thanks to Gabrielle Mander
Compiled and edited by David Sinden
Designed by Robert Walster

First published in Great Britain in 2001 by Buster Books,
an imprint of Mary Ford Publications Ltd,
a subsidiary of Michael O'Mara Holdings,
9 Lion Yard, Tremadoc Road,
London SW4 7NQ, UK.

A CIP catalogue record for this book is available from the British Library

ISBN 1-903840-13-9

1 3 5 7 9 10 8 6 4 2

Visit our website at www.mombooks.com

Made and printed in Great Britain by Bemrose Security Printing, Derby

THE WICKED BOOK OF

txtj0x

Buster Books

Contents

RU a texter?

Text messaging is the way smart people keep in touch using a new language of letters, symbols and numbers to create shorthand messages. It's a great way to send jokes to friends on your mobile phone and by e-mail too. So don't kid around, become a text joker!

Keep it secret

Texting is the ideal way to send secret information, because people can't hear you when you type! We don't recommend it of course, but we understand that it has replaced passing notes in class as a way of commenting on the fascinating lesson and making your classmates laugh.

Lower phone bills

Text messaging is cheap for you and your friends. You don't spend hours on the phone chatting, and it's cheaper than typing all your messages in full. The fewer letters you use without spaces between words, the speedier and less expensive your messages are to send and receive.

Get texting

It's easy to get texting. Although mobile phones vary, they all have a messaging service and it's simple to use.

First steps

1. On your phone's keypad, open your menu of options.
2. Scroll to "Messages" and select it.
3. In the Messages menu you will find an option called something like "Create" or "Message Editor". Having selected this option, you should be ready to start typing your message.

Writing in text

Use the letters, numbers, punctuation marks and symbols shown on the keys to write your message.

Each key represents more than one letter and symbol, and you can use both capital letters and little letters.

You'll need to press a key repeatedly until the letter you want appears. When it does, press the # key to stop the letter flashing and move on to the next letter.

When your text message is complete, press OK to send it.

Be aware

Text messaging is meant to be fun, but be safe.

- Always make sure that you know the person who you are text messaging, and never make arrangements to meet people you don't know.
- Text messaging is a cheap way of using your mobile phone, but don't get carried away and risk a huge telephone bill.
- Don't send really rude messages. People will know who they are from and, anyway, you should respect your friends.

Emoticons

Emoticons

Before mastering the art of text joking you may wish to familiarise yourself with "emoticons". Emoticons are a form of shorthand that uses pictures. Made from letters, numbers and punctuation marks, they can be keyed in seconds and are particularly useful when sending or responding to jokes.

The basic smiley face :-) is a colon, a dash and a close bracket. When you rotate it through 90° it beomes a smile. Most emoticons rotate through 90° although some can be viewed front on.

Take a look at these jokers' emoticons:

:-)))	ha ha ha
;-)	nice one
C=:-)	laughing my head off
+-:-0	dying laughing
:-@	shrieking with laughter
_/<	falling off my chair
:/)	cracking up

‘,-o.....	wetting myself
#:+)	I'm in stitches
,^)___S:-)	tickled pink
:-oo	you're such a hoot
:-’’’!	smokin'
:^,)”	a fit of the giggles
;-,	snigger
;^g	grinning
;^)@’’	rolling on the floor

::--)) doubled up with laughter

(-.-) a side splitter (full on)

(*_*) beaming (full on)

0_*___*_0 grinning from ear to ear (full on)

0 @@ 0 heard it before (full on)

<:-| dumb joke

;^|+) no laughing matter

;^|/) having a humour bypass

You may also wish to use emoticons within your jokes, to describe animals, people or objects. Here are some examples which you'll find later in the book:

8^	chicken
:@)	pig
6U)	elephant
<:>==	turkey
>-^);>	fish
}:-X	cat
:-I=	vampire
B-)	sunglasses
3:-o	cow

Top txt tips

- The trick to texting is to use as few letters and spaces as possible.
- Make words as short as you can. For example, weekend becomes Wknd.
- Start each word with a capital letter.
- Substitute words with single letters or numbers. For example, you becomes U.
- A capital letter also means a long sound in a word. So, baby becomes BAB.
- A capital letter can mean a double letter, so bubble becomes BuBl.
- Don't confuse a capital 'I' with a small 'l' — on some phones these look the same.

Texters' essentials

Here are some essential short cuts and abbreviations you'll find in this book:

B	be
Bcos	because
Bf	boyfriend
B4	before
C	see
Dnsr	dinosaur
K	a thousand
L8r	later

No	know or no
NE1	anyone
NEthng	anything
Pls	please
R	are
Str8	straight
T	the
Thru	through
U	you
UR	you are
Wot	what

W8rW8r	waiter, waiter
W/	with
Ya	you, or your
x	cross
2	to, too, two
2gtha	together
?UGt	what do you get?
?UCALA	what do you call a?
4	for, four
$	ss
@	at
"[.	knock, knock
?[.	who's there?

?UGt
What do you get?

?UGt

What do you get if you cross
a spider with a computer?
?UGt IfUxASpdrW/ACmputa
A web page.
AWebPAg

What do you get if you cross a
cow with a map?
?UGt IfUxA3:-oW/AMap
Udderly lost.
UDrlELst

What do you get if you cross
a zebra with a pelican?
?UGt IfUxAZbraW/APeliCn
Across the street safely.
AxTStrEtSAfly

What do you get if you cross
a chicken with a monster?
?UGt IfUxA8^W/AMnsta
Free strange eggs.
FrEStrAngEGs

What do you get if you cross a bridge with a car?

?UGt IfUxABrdgW/ACA

To the other side of the river.

2TOthaSIdOfTRiva

What do you get if you cross a kangaroo with a sweater?

?UGt IfUxAKngrOW/ASweta

A wooly jumper.

AWOlyJmpa

What do you get if you cross a car park with a safari park?
?UGt IfUxACAPrkW/ASfriPrk
Double yellow lions.
DbleYloLions

What do you get if you cross a sheep with a radiator?
?UGt IfUxAShEpW/ARAdiata
Central bleating.
CntrlBlEtin

What do you get if you cross a skunk with a table-tennis bat?
?UGt IfUxASkunkW/ATblTeNisBt
Pong pong.
PongPong

What do you get if you cross a skeleton with a dog?
?UGt IfUxASkltonW/ADg
An animal that buries itself.
AnAnmlThtBerEsItslf

What do you get if you cross a mouse with an olive?

?UGt IfUxAMseW/AnOliv

A squeak that oils itself.

ASqEkThtOilsItslf

What do you get if you cross a toadstool with a wardrobe?

?UGt IfUxATdstOlW/AWrdrOb

Not mushroom for your clothes.

NtMushrOm4YaClOths

What do you get if you cross a computer with a potato?

?UGt IfUxACmputaW/APtato

Microchips.

Mcrochps

What do you get if you cross a biscuit with a truck?

?UGt IfUxABscitW/ATruc

Crumbs.

Crmbs

SpOKE

Spooky

SpOkE

When can't you bury people in a graveyard?
WenCntUBerEPpleInAGrAvyd?
When they're not dead.
WenThyRNtDed

Why are graveyards always noisy?
YRGrAvydsAlwysNoisE?
Because of the coffin.
BcosOfTCoFn

What do you call a ghost's father and mother?

?UCALA GOstsPa&Ma?

Transparents.

TransPArnts

What roads do ghosts live on?

WotRdsDoGOstsLivOn?

Dead ends.

DedEnds

Why did the car stop for the ghost?
YDdTCaStp4TGOst?
It had a nervous breakdown.
ItHdANrvsBrkdwn

What position do ghosts play in football?
WotPositnDoGOstsPlAInFOtbL?
Ghoulie.
GhooLE

What did the ghost say to her son?
WotDidTGOstSA2HrSn?
Don't spook until you're spooken to.
DntSpOkUntIURSpOkn2

What flavour ice cream do vampires like?
WotFlAValcCrEmDo:-i=sLIk?
Veinilla.
VeiniLa

What instrument does a skeleton play?

WotInstrmntDosASkltnPlA?

Trombone.

Trmbone

Who does a vampire fall in love with?

HODosA:-I=FLInLuvW/?

The girl necks door.

TGrlNeksDOr

Why didn't the skeleton go to the party?
YDdntTSkltnGo2TParT?
She had no body to go with.
SheHdNoBdy2GoW/

What did the skeleton say to her boyfriend?
WotDdTSkltnSA2HrBf?
I love every bone in your body.
ILuvEvrEBOnInYaBodE

How do you make a milkshake?
HowDoUMAkAMilkshAk?
Sneak up behind it and say "Boo!".
SnEkUpBhndIt&SABO!

Why are ghosts afraid?
YRGOstsAfrd?
Because they've got no guts.
BcosThyvGtNoGuts

Why do demons like ghouls?
YDoDmonsLkeGOls?
Because demons are a ghoul's best friend.
BcosDmonsRAGOlsBstFrnd

Dnsrs
Dinosaurs

Dnsrs

What followed the dinosaurs?
WotFLwdTDnsrs?
Their tails.
TherTAls

What's as big as a dinosaur but weighs nothing?
WotsAsBgAsADnsrBtWAs0?
Its shadow.
ItsShdw

What do you get when a dinosaur sneezes?
?UGt WenADnsrSnEzs
Out of the way.
OutOfTWA

How do you know if there's a dinosaur in your refrigerator?
HowDoUNoIfThersADnsrIn YaFrdge?
Look for footprints in the pizza.
LOk4FOtprntsInTPiZa

What do you get when you cross a dinosaur with a bomb?

?UGt WenUxADnsrW/ABom

Dinomite.

DnOmIte

What does a Tyrannosaurus eat?

WotDosATiraNosrusEt?

Anything she wants to.

NEthngSheWans2

What should you do if you find
a dinosaur in your bed?
WotShldUDoIfUFndADnsrInYaBd?
Sleep somewhere else.
SlEpSumwerEls

Do you know how long dinosaurs
walked the planet?
DoUNoHwLngDnsrsWlkdTPlnt?
Exactly the same as short dinosaurs.
XactLTSAmAsShrtDnsrs

What do you get if you cross a dinosaur with a pig?

?UGt IfUxADnsrW/A:@)

Jurassic Pork.

Jra$icPork

What do you call a dinosaur who's been left in the rain?

?UCALA DnsrHOsBnLftInTRAn

A Stegosaurust.

AStgosrust

Why do dinosaurs eat raw meat?
YDoDnsrsEtRwMEt?
Because they don't know how to cook.
BcosThyDntNoHw2COk

What do you call a dinosaur with no eyes?
?UCALA DnsrW/0iis
A Doyouthinkhesaurus.
ADoYaThnkHeSrUs

What does a Triceratops sit on?
WotDsATrcratpsSitOn?
Its Tricera-bottom.
ItsTrcraBoTm

Why are there old dinosaur bones in the museum?
YRTherOldDnsrBnesInTMusEm?
Because they can't afford new ones.
BcosThyCntAFrdNu1s

YDdT8^xTRd?

Why did the chicken cross the road?

YDdT8^xTRd?

Why did the chicken cross the road?
YDdT8^xTRd?
To get to the other side.
2Gt2TOthaSId

Why did the chewing gum cross the road?
YDdTChwnGmxTRd?
Because it was stuck to the chicken.
BcosItWosStk2T8^

Why didn't the chicken cross the road?

YDdntT8^xTRd?

Because he lost his guts.

BcosHLstHsGuts

Why did the chicken surf the net?

YDdT8^SrfTNet?

To get to the other site.

2Gt2TOthaSIt

Why did the chicken cross the playground?
YDdT8^xTPlAgrnd?
To get to the other slide.
2Gt2TOthaSLId

Why did the turkey cross the road?
YDdT<:>==xTRd?
To prove he wasn't chicken.
2PrOvHWosnt8^

Why did the dinosaur cross the road?

YDdTDnsrxTRd?

Because chickens hadn't evolved yet.

Bcos8^sHdntEvlvdYt

Why did the chicken cross the road twice?

YDdT8^xTRd2yys?

Because he was a dirty double-crosser.

BcosHeWosADrtyDblexr

Why did the cow cross the road?
YDdT3:-oxTRd?
To get to the udder side.
2Gt2TUDrSId

W8rW8r

Waiter, waiter

W8rW8r

Waiter, waiter, what's wrong with this fish?

W8rW8r WotsRongW/Ths>-^);>?

Long time, no sea.

LngTImNoC

Waiter, waiter, this soup tastes funny.

W8rW8r ThsSOpTAstsFNE

Then why aren't you laughing?

ThnYArntU:-)))?

Waiter, waiter, bring some food, and make it snappy.
W8rW8r
BrngSumFOd&MAkItSnaPE
How about a crocodile sandwich, sir?
HowAbtACrcdleSndwchSr?

Waiter, waiter, do you have frog's legs?
W8rW8r DoUHveFrgsLgs?
No, I always walk like this.
NoIAlwAsWlkLIkThs

Waiter, waiter, there's a small caterpillar in this salad.
W8rW8r ThsASmL}:-XrpLrInThsSald
Would you like me to get you a bigger one?
WIdULIKMe2GetUABGa1?

Waiter, waiter, this egg is bad.
W8rW8r ThsEGIsBd
Don't blame me, I only laid the table.
DntBlAmMeIOnlELAdTTble

Waiter, waiter, what's this fly doing in my soup?
W8rW8r
WotsThsFlyDoinInMySOp?
The backstroke, sir.
TBkstrkSr

Waiter, waiter, do you serve snails?
W8rW8r DoUSrvSnAls?
Sit down, sir, we serve anyone.
SitDwnSrWeSrvNE1

Waiter, waiter, is there soup on the menu?

W8rW8r IsThrSOpOnTMnu?

No, madam I wiped it off.

NoMdmIWIpdItOF

Waiter, waiter, there's a fly in my wine.

W8rW8r ThrsAFlyInMyWIn

You asked for something with a little body in it.

UAskd4SumnW/ALTleBdyInIt

Waiter, waiter, there's a fly in my custard.
W8rW8r ThrsAFlyInMyCstrd
I'll fetch him a spoon, sir.
ILFtchHmASpOnSr

Waiter, waiter, my lunch is talking to me.
W8rW8r MyLnchIsTlkn2Me
Well you did ask for a tongue sandwich.
WeLUDidAsk4ATungSndwch

Waiter, waiter, there's a fly in the butter.

W8rW8r ThrsAFlyInTBTa

Yes madam, it's a butterfly.

YesMdmItsABTaFly

Waiter, waiter, there's a dead fly in my soup.

W8rW8r
ThrsADedFlyInMySOp.

Oh no, who will look after his family.

ONoHOWiLLOKAftaHsFmIE

’’[.

Knock, knock

’’[. Knock, knock

Knock, knock	’’[.
Who's there?	.[?
Albert	**Albert**
Albert who?	**AlbertHO?**

Albert you'll never guess.

AlbertULNυrGe$

Knock, knock ''[.

Who's there? .[?

Alex **Alex**

Alex who? **AlexHO?**

Alexplain later, just let me in.

AlexplAnL8rJstLtMeIn

Knock, knock	''[.
Who's there?	**.[?**
Luke	**Luke**
Luke who?	**LukeHO?**

Luke through the keyhole
and you'll see.

LukeThruTKEhle&ULC

Knock, knock	''[.
Who's there?	.[?
Stan	**Stan**
Stan who?	**StanHO?**

Stan back, I'm going to break the door down.

StanBckImGoNaBrkTDOrDwn

Knock, knock	**"[.**
Who's there?	**.[?**
Daniel	**Daniel**
Daniel who?	**DanielHO?**

Daniel at me, it's not my fault.

Daniel@MeItsNtMyFlt

Knock, knock ''[.

Who's there? .[?

De Niro **DeNiro**

De Niro who? **DeNiroHO**

De Niro you get, the uglier you look.

DeNiroUGtTUglrULOk

Knock, knock ''[.

Who's there? .[?

Seymour **Seymour**

Seymour who? **SeymourHO?**

Seymour if you look through the window.

SeymourIfULOkThrUTWndw

?UCALA
What do you call a?

?UCALA

What do you call a kangaroo at the North Pole?
?UCALA KngrO@TNrthPle
Lost.
Lst

What do you call a small parent?
?UCALA SmLPArnt
A minimum.
AMniMm

What do you call a pen with no hair?
?UCALA PenW/NoHair
A bald point.
ABldPnt <:-)

What do you call a man with no underpants?
?UCALA MnW/0UndrPnts
Nicholas.
Nicolas

What do you call a man with a tree on his head?
?UCALA MnW/ATrEOnHsHed
EdWood.
EdWOd

What do you call a friend with an elephant on his head?
?UCALA FrndW/An6U)OnHsHed
A flatmate.
AFlatmAt

What do you call a woman who steals cows?

?UCALA WmnHOStels3:-Os

A beef burglar.

ABEfBurglr

What do you call a failed lion tamer?

?UCALA FAldLionTmr

Claude Bottom.

ClaudBoTm

What do you call an unlucky cat?
?UCALAn Unluky}:-X
A catastrophe.
A}:-XastrOfe

What do you call a sheep that says Quack?
?UCALA ShEpThtSezQak?
Bilingual.
Bilngwl

What do you call a woman with one leg?
?UCALA WmnW/1Lg
Eileen.
ILEn

What do you call a woman crossing a river?
?UCALA WmnxnARivr
Bridget.
Brdgt

What do you call a camel with no humps?

?UCALA CamlW/0Hmps

A horse.

AHrs

What do you call a lady in the distance?

?UCALA LdyInTDstnce

Dot.

Dot

2C0I4SkOI

Too cool for school

2COl4SkOl

What's a mushroom?
WotsAMshrOm?
Where the school food is stored.
WhrTSkOlFOdIsStOrd

Did you hear about the cross-eyed teacher?
DdUHErAbtTxiidTecha?
She couldn't control her pupils.
SheCldntCntrlHrPupls

What came after the Stone Age?
WotCAmAftaTStnAg?
The sausage.
TSosij

What's the difference between school gravy and frogspawn?
WotsTDFrnsBtwEnSkOlGrvy &Frgsporn?
Not a lot
NtALt.

Why did the dinner lady get an electric shock?

YDdTDNrLADGtAnElctrcShk?

She stepped on a bun and a current went up her leg.

SheStePdOnABun&ACuRnt WntUpHrLg

Why does my teacher wear sunglasses?

YDosMyTechaWerB-)?

Because I am so bright.

BcosImSoBrIt

What's the longest word?
WotsTLngstWrd?
Smiles - because there is a mile between the first and last letters.
:-)s BcosThersAMIL BtwEnT1st&LstLeTrs

Where is the best place for the school sickroom?
WersTBstPlAc4TSkOlSckrOm?
Next to the canteen.
Nxt2TCntEn

What's the longest sentence?
WotsTLngstSntnce?
Life imprisonment.
LIfImprsnmnt

Be sure that you go straight home!
BSurThtUGoStr8HOm!
I can't, I live around the corner.
ICntILivArndTCrnr

Laugh and the class laughs with you.
:-)))&TCla$:-)))sW/U
But you get detention alone!
BtUGtDtntnAlOn!

What is the best way to get straight 'A's?
WotsTBstWA2GtStr8As?
Use a ruler.
UsARlr

Who invented fractions?
HOInuntdFrctns?
Henry the 1/8.
HnryT8th

What's the difference between an American school and an English school?
WotsTDffrnceBtwEnAUSSkOl &AUKSkOl?
About 3000 miles.
Abt3KMILs

DrDr

Doctor, doctor

DrDr

Doctor, doctor, I think I'm invisible.
DrDr IThnkImInvsble
Who said that?
HOSdTht?

Doctor, doctor, I keep getting smaller.
DrDr IKEpGetnSmLr
You'll just have to be a little patient.
UlJstHve2BALTIPAtnt

Doctor, doctor, I think I'm a ghost.
DrDr IThnkImAGOst
Whatever's possessed you?
WhteursPoedU?

Doctor, doctor, I feel like a pair of curtains.
DrDr IFEILIkAPrOfCrtns
Pull yourself together.
PuLYaslf2gtha

Doctor, doctor, everyone keeps ignoring me.
DrDr Evry1KEpsIgnrnMe
Next please.
NxtPlse

Doctor, doctor, I keep thinking there are two of me.
DrDr IKEpThnknTherR2OfMe
One at a time please.
1@ATImPlse

Doctor, doctor, I can't get to sleep.
DrDr ICntGt2SlEp
Sit on the edge of the bed and you'll soon drop off.
StOnTEdgOfTBed&ULSOnDrpOF

Doctor, doctor, I feel like a pack of cards.
DrDr IFEILIKAPckOfCrds
I'll deal with you later
ILDEIW/UL8r

Doctor, doctor, my eye hurts when I drink tea.

DrDr MyIHrtsWenIDrnkT

Take the spoon out.

TAkTSpOnOut

Doctor, doctor, I feel like a needle.

DrDr IFEILIkANEdl

I see your point.

ICYaPnt

Doctor, doctor, you have to help me out.
DrDr UHav2HlpMeOut
Certainly, which way did you come in?
CrtnlEWichWADdUCumIn?

Doctor, doctor, I'm a burglar.
DrDr ImABrglr
Have you taken anything for it?
HavUTAknNEthn4It?

Doctor, doctor, I keep thinking
I'm a vampire.
DrDr IKEpThnknImA:-I=
Necks please.
NeksPls

Doctor, doctor, I've broken my arm
in two places.
DrDr IvBrknMyArmIn2PlAcs
Well don't go back there again.
WeLDntGoBakTherAgn

Ova2U
Over to you

Ova2U

Why not jot down some of your own favourite jokes in text, or have a go at making up some personalised emoticons?

Ova2U

Ovа2U

Wan2Hlp?

People are inventing text jokes and emoticons all the time, so we are constantly adding to our files to keep right up to date. If you and your friends use any text jokes or emoticons that aren't in this book or you think up some brilliant ones yourself, let us know about them.

E-mail us at:

jokes@michaelomarabooks.com

We'll let you know if your suggestions are going to be included.

Thanks

Other titles

You can order other little books directly from Buster Books, all at £1.99 each including postage (UK only):

The Wicked Book of Txt Tlk ISBN 1-903840-12-0

The Little Book of Secret Codes ISBN 1-903840-15-5

The Little Book of The Pocket Magician ISBN 1-903840-16-3

Postage and packaging outside the UK:
Europe: add 20% of retail price
Rest of the world: add 30% of retail price

To order any Buster Books, call our credit-card hotline on 020 8324 5652